April Cornell
Decorating with Color

April Cornell
Decorating with Color

STERLING PUBLISHING CO., INC. NEW YORK
A STERLING/CHAPELLE BOOK

Chapelle, Ltd.:
Jo Packham, Sara Toliver, Cindy Stoeckl
Art Director: Karla Haberstich
Copy Editor: Marilyn Goff
Staff: Kelly Ashkettle, Areta Bingham, Anne Bruns, Donna Chambers, Emily Frandsen, Lana Hall, Susan Jorgensen, Jennifer Luman, Melissa Maynard, Barbara Milburn, Lecia Monsen, Suzy Skadburg, Kim Taylor, Linda Venditti, Desirée Wybrow

If you have any questions or comments, please contact:
Chapelle, Ltd., Inc., P.O. Box 9252, Ogden, UT 84409
(801) 621-2777 · (801) 621-2788 Fax
e-mail: chapelle@chapelleltd.com
web site: www.chapelleltd.com

A Red Lips 4 Courage Book
Eileen Cannon Paulin, President, Rebecca Ittner, Catherine Risling

Red Lips 4 Courage Communications, Inc.
8502 E. Chapman Ave., 303
Orange, CA 92869
e-mail: rl4courage@redlips4courage.com
web site: www.redlips4courage.com

Graphic design of book interior:
Deborah Kehoe, Kehoe+Kehoe Design Associates, Inc., Burlington, VT

Library of Congress Cataloging-in-Publication Data

Cornell, April.
April Cornell Decorating with Color.
p. cm.
"A Sterling/Chapelle Book."
Includes index.
ISBN 1-4027-1613-3
1. Color in interior decortion. I. Title: Decorating with color. II. Title.
NK2115.5.C6C69 2004
747'.94--dc22
2004005251

10 9 8 7 6 5 4 3 2 1
Published by Sterling Publishing Co., Inc.
387 Park Avenue South, New York, NY 10016
©2004 by April Cornell
Distributed in Canada by Sterling Publishing
c/o Canadian Manda Group, One Atlantic Avenue, Suite 105
Toronto, Ontario, Canada M6K 3E7
Distributed in Great Britain by Chrysalis Books Group PLC,
The Chrysalis Building, Bramley Road, London W10 6SP, England
Distributed in Australia by Capricorn Link (Australia) Pty. Ltd.
P.O. Box 704, Windsor, NSW 2756, Australia
Printed and Bound in China
All Rights Reserved
Sterling ISBN 1-4027-1613-3

Dedication

To my men,

Chris, Cameron, Lee and Kelly, and all our days together.

To my women,

My mother Florence Janbroers and my mother-in-law Mary Cornell.

As women do, we do, as women are, we are.

Together you inspire me to be the woman of my family.

Contents

■ ■ ■ ■

Meet April Cornell

Lifelong artist April Cornell has always been inspired by the colors of nature. For nearly 30 years, she has beautifully translated her artful combinations of color and floral designs into exquisite collections of romantic clothing, linens and home accessories.

Her creativity was nurtured by her parents and family during her upbringing in Montreal, Canada. While studying Fine Arts at Dawson College, she met her husband and business partner Chris Cornell. Their partnership is a dynamic combination of creativity and business savvy. While traveling the world together in flower-child style, they began importing fabrics and clothing, which they sold in a small upstairs shop in Montreal.

Soon April was designing their own lines and the business blossomed into over 110 April Cornell and La Cache boutiques in North America and a wholesale company, Cornell Trading. With design and manufacturing facilities in New Delhi, India, and China and sources in Indonesia, the Cornells continue to travel the world in search of inspiration from the people, art and beauty of the many places they visit.

April and Chris share many passions including caring for the people in the company's main production area in India. They actively support the Concern India Foundation and have founded the Giving World Foundation, which helps the underprivileged in India. The foundations fund many programs including schools, programs to empower women, and help impoverished children living in ghettos and on the streets.

inviting environment of rich color, luxurious textures and ultra-feminine styles.

The Cornells have three sons, Cameron, Lee and Kelly. Having been raised in the colorful international world of Cornell, Cameron founded Kit Cornell, a unique line of casual clothing for men and women.

Cornell Trading also funds the Gali Schools, small outdoor schools that allow the children of the streets to become the first generation of their families to read and write.

The Cornells have an uncanny ability to connect emotionally with their customers, based on April's designing with the intent of allowing women to free their spirit in an

Lee is a journalist based in New Mexico, and Kelly recently completed a documentary on the Gali Schools while completing his high school studies. When they are not traveling, they divide their time between operations in India, Hong Kong, Montreal and their home in Burlington, Vermont.

April and Chris' philosophy of making an occasion of everyday life appears seemingly simple, yet it is what makes everything they do distinctively special. Who better to walk you through the wonderful world of colorful living than April Cornell?

Introduction

My dear friends,

When my husband Chris suggested that I do a book on color, I admit I was a bit flummoxed—what did he mean? Why talk about color? Well, a little research showed me there were more than enough reasons to talk about color. One reason is there seems to be a lot of mystery and intimidation around color. What is a natural decorating ally has grown into an intimidating science. People have become afraid of using color and of making mistakes with color. Oh, alas, being graded on our choices. Will comparing and judging never stop? When I spoke with my mother, a lifelong decorator, about doing a book on color, her comment was that 90 percent of people are afraid of color. Ninety percent, well that doesn't leave very many color-confident people.

When I asked her who these people were worried about pleasing, she said they want their friends to be impressed when they visit. "I love your colors" is high praise.

So, my friends, this book will try and help you win that praise—after all, that does seem to be a goal—but in winning that praise you will win your own praise; you will impress yourself. You can't actually impress someone else if you do not feel confident and satisfied with your choices. Using color and learning about color is not a static or ever completed activity. I would describe it as a hobby, potentially lifelong, that will expand its influence and grow in interest the more it is used. I love things that increase in value as they are used, rather than diminish with use, don't you?

Some people see the world in black and white, some see it as a world of outlines and silhouettes; they haven't actually noticed the colors, but I see the world in a broad spectrum of color that is varied, rich and embracing. Experiencing color in the world is like adding dimensions of interest to your life. It is adding layers of value to an activity as simple as looking.

Do you remember the childhood game of 'I Spy' where you had to find a color (usually an obscure one)? Well, that game really made you look for colors. It made you notice just how many reds might be in a room or how many different blues there were. It forced your eye to distinguish colors from each other and to pick out colors. Learning about color is a bit like 'I Spy.' You are looking for common colors and their links. You are looking at colors and understanding the relationship between one color and another. You are immersing yourself in color. In this book, I will encourage you to get up close to color, to experiment with it, and to acknowledge the color in your life that is already there.

Many people live with others and must adjust their tastes to the family tastes. You can learn how to use different palettes to give a more masculine room, and be as artful in your own room as you are in a child's. Do you have a room of refuge, a quiet spot, for your activities? If you do, you will find this room an important one to practice your color ideas.

In this book, I deliberately tried to use different locations for showing color ideas. There is an old chalet on a Quebec lake, there is a beach house in the Cayman Islands, and there is a charming cottage in Southern California. Each of these locations is inspiring in its natural color palette. These palettes travel well around the country, and if you want to create a California palette in a home in Minnesota, you can. And if bright Cayman colors enliven a Toronto apartment, then that is sun in the winter.

Use color to make the north into the south, the south into the north, and use color to take your own patch of nature and bring it inside. Use color for variety, for creating moods and for living a life of richness. Use color to help you live fully and expressively in your home and in your activities. Use color for happiness.

All the best,

Chapter One

Seeing Color
in Nature

Our natural surroundings are an integral part of us. Nature, like our own language, weaves her way through our whole life. From the words we speak to the air we breathe, nature is what we are made of. Think of our language and how natural items have come to represent colors and our way of seeing color. We use words that are the names of fruits, flowers and foods to describe color; we use nighttime to talk about dark color and a sunny day to describe everything from mood to yellow. Color and nature are threaded through human expression so intimately that we may become blissfully unaware of the origin of our talk. Colors like peach, lavender, midnight blue, apple green, earth, terra-cotta, rust, orange and ivory, all are commonly used and each conjures up an image of color based on a natural reference.

Flowers, fruits, earth, our language and our speech are full of references to nature and color. Complexions can be rosy like the pink of a delicate rose or blooming like a healthy flower. Eyes can sparkle like water in a fast-moving stream. Nature is, of course, the origin of color.

Let nature guide you and stimulate you in your choice of color. One of the interesting things about nature is she loves to mix colors. If you copy nature, you will never have to worry about colors matching. Hers don't!

Thank you Mother Nature—you make decorating so much easier and more fun. I always refer to nature as "she." Mother Nature, after all, is her formal name. Her creativity, unstoppable productivity and the

OPPOSITE PAGE: *A lakeside boathouse with quilts airing on a summer day.*

Nature Wheel
autumn

Maple

If you are inclined to think of a forest being only green and brown, take a closer look. Numerous other colors abound.

forest

birch

gold

autumn ivory

olives

Rust to Red

giving birth every spring to newness and freshness is so patently female that I enjoy saying "she." I am very proud of Mother Nature and I would like her to feel satisfaction in how I use her gifts, too.

There is much to be said about using nature as a guide for choosing color. There is a forward and backwards response to nature. Nature can inspire you with her many colors and help you to put colors together, or you can add nature into your environment by picking out colors of your room and finding them in nature.

An easy way to understand nature's palettes is to go outside and join her. If you live in an area where there are trees, meadows, flowers, woods, pastures or gardens, this will be easy to do. If you have none of these nearby, you will have to go to the market or flower shop (botanical gardens are wonderful). A supermarket can provide access to fruits and vegetables year-round, which can be used to pick up color accents for your table.

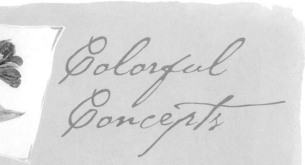

Colorful Concepts

The colors of nature coordinate. They belong together and they go well side by side, but they don't match. To join my world of color and to enjoy color, you will have to set aside matching colors and take up mixing colors.

Thank you Mother Nature —you make decorating so much easier and more fun.

Field guides and books on places and nature found at a bookstore or library can also be helpful.

In order to be truly guided by nature in your color selections, you have to get up and go! Give yourself a specific project. Leaves, shapes, colors, flowers and patterns can all be found outdoors, waiting to be studied and to inspire you.

Harvest Palette

highlights

accents for walls + background

breathe color

break up color

spicy colors

forest green

dark teal green

olive family

Going outside "to look at nature" is a rather large task. It's hard to bring home the sky and the mountains, so break this activity into smaller portions with a specific goal and you will find that nature responds with her own unexpected twists and turns.

LEFT: *This collection of gourds and fall chrysanthemums on a pine sideboard are embellished with "uzbeki" embroideries. Note the framed block-printed textile behind the sideboard.*

OPPOSITE PAGE: *Taking time to relax and enjoy nature is the best inspiration for learning about color. Settled below a tree, this comfy spot on the forest floor is ideal for looking at color, studying nature and taking a replenishing break.*

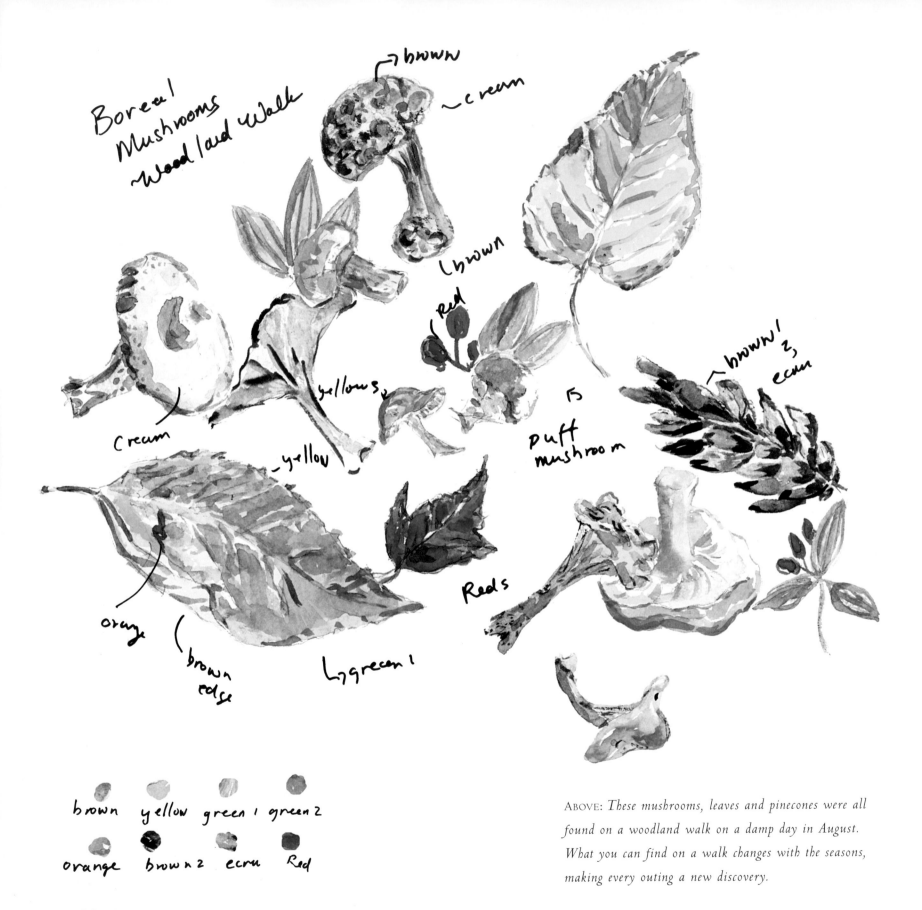

Boreal
Mushrooms
Woodland Walk

brown

cream

brown

Red

brown 1,
ecru

cream

yellow₃

yellow

puff
mushroom

15

orange

brown
edge

green 1

Reds

brown

yellow

green1

green2

orange

brown 2

ecru

Red

ABOVE: *These mushrooms, leaves and pinecones were all found on a woodland walk on a damp day in August. What you can find on a walk changes with the seasons, making every outing a new discovery.*

Examples of a few small goals for nature walks:

WOODLAND WALK IN THE FALL

Locate maple leaves in five different colors. Find other leaves of different shapes that grow near the maple tree, such as birch and oak. Note the colors of the tree trunks, stems and leaves. Notice how the leaves are not a single color, how a green leaf may have sharp shades of yellow. It might have different colors at the edges. The stem may be reddish with streaks of green. A maple may be orange sprinkled with yellow and green. Reds may nearly look wine heavy and dark, almost purple.

Leaf peepers—those curious souls who invade the countryside during the changing of the leaves—understand the autumn palette; it is a palette composed of leaves, hills and grasses of different colors.

MEADOW WALK

Walk through a meadow and pick grasses and sedges. You may find milkweed. Note the sages, ivories and almost blue greens of a single pod. See the soft yellow color inside of

A Quest for Beauty

Collect your leaves on a canvas or in an attractive canvas tote, or carry a notebook to place leaves inside or to note details that interest you. A digital camera is a good tool for capturing color that doesn't fit in your pocket or bag.

About the canvas or printed bag: I do believe you should use something attractive and pleasing. It is not good to start your quest for beauty with something that is the antithesis of that. You will learn in this book that letting the right things into your environment is an important part of learning how to select color. Narrowing your choices at this early stage of color selection is what thinking like a colorist, a designer, a decorator and an artist is all about.

Collection bag

Points of Inspiration

I have a longtime friend in India, who is in the same trade—garments and design. She refers to ideas—no matter how humble—as the points of inspiration. I have adopted these words in my own speech and understand that the takeoff point for any new idea has a point of inspiration. This starting point—this point of inspiration—no matter how small or how far from the final product, is essential; ideas need beginnings. Be open to beginnings.

Was there something on your walk you didn't set out to find? Nuts, seeds, moss, berries—these are all good accents. Were there berries nestled in the leaves or was a rare white trillium in its short-lived spring showing waiting for you? Did you notice that the stems and veins of leaves and bushes contained more colors than you thought? Make a note of what strikes your fancy. Enjoy the accidental encounters that can be the points of inspiration for your thinking.

A longtime friend refers to ideas—no matter how humble—as the points of inspiration.

the pod. What is growing near the milkweed? Does it look good next to the milkweed color? Is it green or bluish? What else do you see? Green? Is it a yellowy green? Are some pods old and browning and, if so, is this a good accent color? Make a note of it for future reference.

MUSHROOM WALK

You'll need a damp spot to find mushrooms; and if you find one, they can be plentiful. Look under leaves, on the side of trees and sprouting from logs. Rock faces can yield both moss and mushrooms. Examine the mushrooms for color, shape, texture and variety. Observe what they grow near—earth, damp leaves, moss. Are all of the items creating a palette of color? Are there colors here to decorate with? Which color would you want to emphasize, and which is only an accent?

Start forming palettes from what you find. The more time you spend looking at color, the more you'll find yourself saying, "Oh, I love that color!" And that is the beginning—defining what you love.

Let nature be your guide,
Let blue skies give bounce gone
Let greens of the forest add depth
Let flowers give the focus —
Let petals and stamens
and buds add faces and
friendship and Love

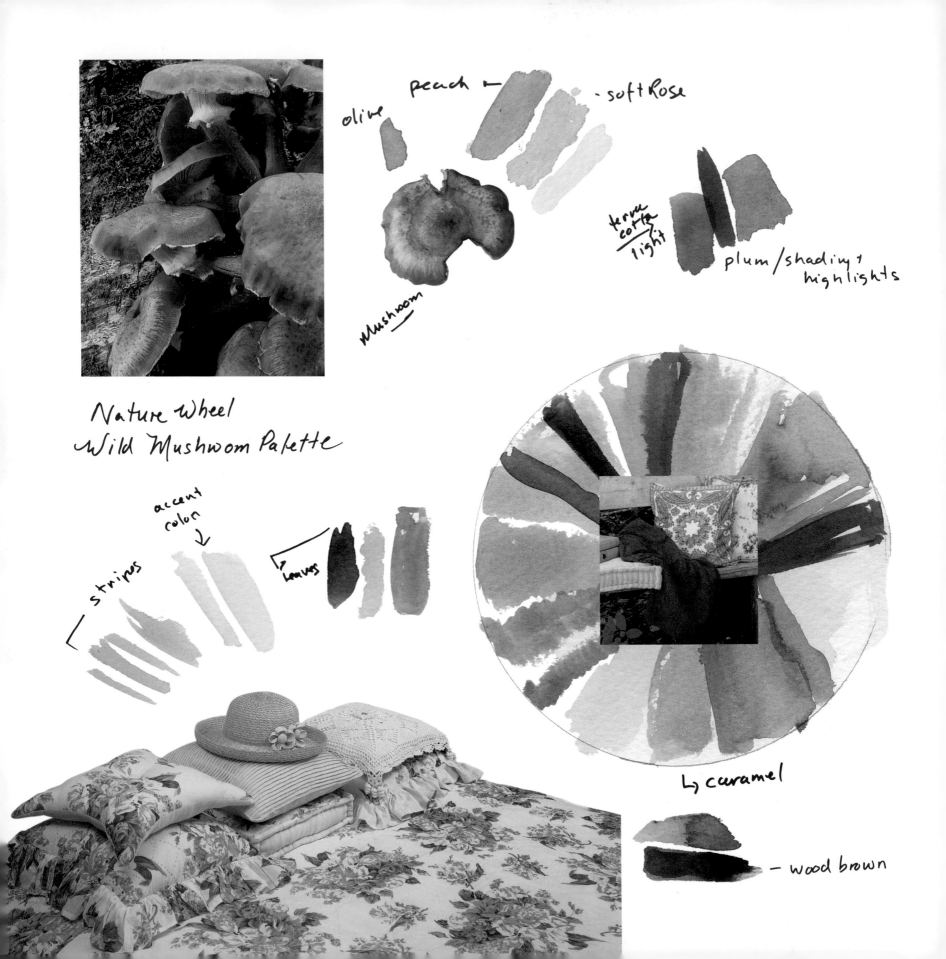

olive

peach

soft Rose

Mushroom

terra cotta light

plum/shading + highlights

Nature Wheel
Wild Mushroom Palette

accent color

stripes

leaves

caramel

wood brown

In a Nutshell

A GIFT OF NATURE

It is likely that something in your discovery walk—a plant or flower—will have touched you in a special way. Surprise a friend with it as a gift and wrap the pot or vase with a pretty napkin. Personalize it with a watercolor initial of her name or a personal message. Carry the nature theme to the table napkin by tying the napkin with a leaf. The blue blossoms and green leaves reflect the colors of the table linens. Evergreen and dried flowers work well.

Chapter Two

Color Basics— Not What You Think

COLOR MEMORY

One way to start thinking about color is to do a little brainstorming about color memories. The way a therapist may encourage one to look back at early memories, to examine life, can also be done to remember when color made its first impact on you. Talking about color makes you more aware of it.

I have an early color memory from when I was a child. It is a memory of a sunset-colored taffeta party dress. This party dress was a combination of violet, soft pink and blue in a shot plaid, all a shimmer with an orchid-colored belt. In a box, it lay—waiting for my mother to iron it so I could go to a party. Patience is not my strongest trait, and at age seven, I decided to iron this extravagance of a dress, this sublimity of color, myself. An iron-scorched hole spoiled that dress. I wore my sister's red suit instead, but I remember its colors perfectly and I remember the red suit too.

Do you have a color memory? Have you ever glimpsed the Caribbean waters and seen a turquoise sea? Did you have a blue sweater that everyone said matched your eyes? Look through your memory. Talk to yourself about color—colors that you notice, color that surprised you, color that called to you and

OPPOSITE PAGE: *This girl's room combines a mint mohair blanket and a pink satin quilt. Both of these have a delightfully soft texture that children love.*

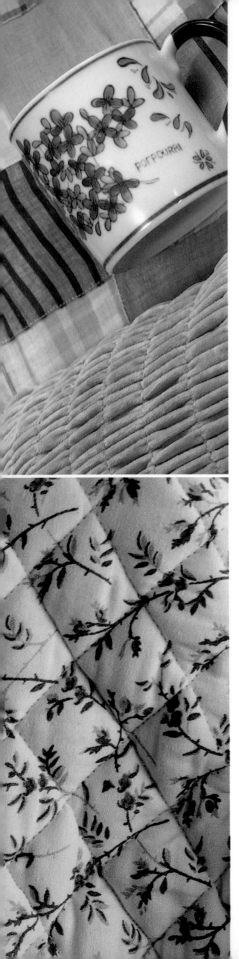

even colors you don't like. Not liking a color can be part of your memories too.

As a child, I loathed pink (imagine!). I didn't care for strawberry ice cream and to me, the color pink was all wrapped up in that ice cream. For years, I was the blue girl and my sister was the pink girl. Eventually, pink found its way back into my life and I now enjoy it for the "emotional" color it is.

When I watch people select a tablecloth, I notice that the first thing that attracts them is the color. If you want a blue tablecloth, a beautiful red one is unlikely to move you. If blue is the color you want, build on blue.

OPPOSITE PAGE: *Blue can be its own palette just using many different shades, and becomes interesting when many different patterns are used.*

APPROACHES TO COLOR

There are two basic steps to building a color palette. First, choose a color you like and build from it by incorporating lighter and darker shades of the color. By using the color in large and small prints, plaids, stripes, solids and textured fabrics, the variety of uses makes it interesting.

Second, add accent. An accent color can animate colors; for example, notice what orange does to brown in a bouquet of flowers. A contrasting throw on a bed, a festive jacket on a hook or a stack of books can pick up the colors of the room. Any element from personal clothing, shoes, blankets, scarves to a bowl of fruit, a teapot or a vase can introduce color into everything.

Look at homes professionally photographed; the incidental items are as important as a part of the décor as the major pieces of furniture. These smaller accents often provide the needed color boost to pull a room together or take it over the top.

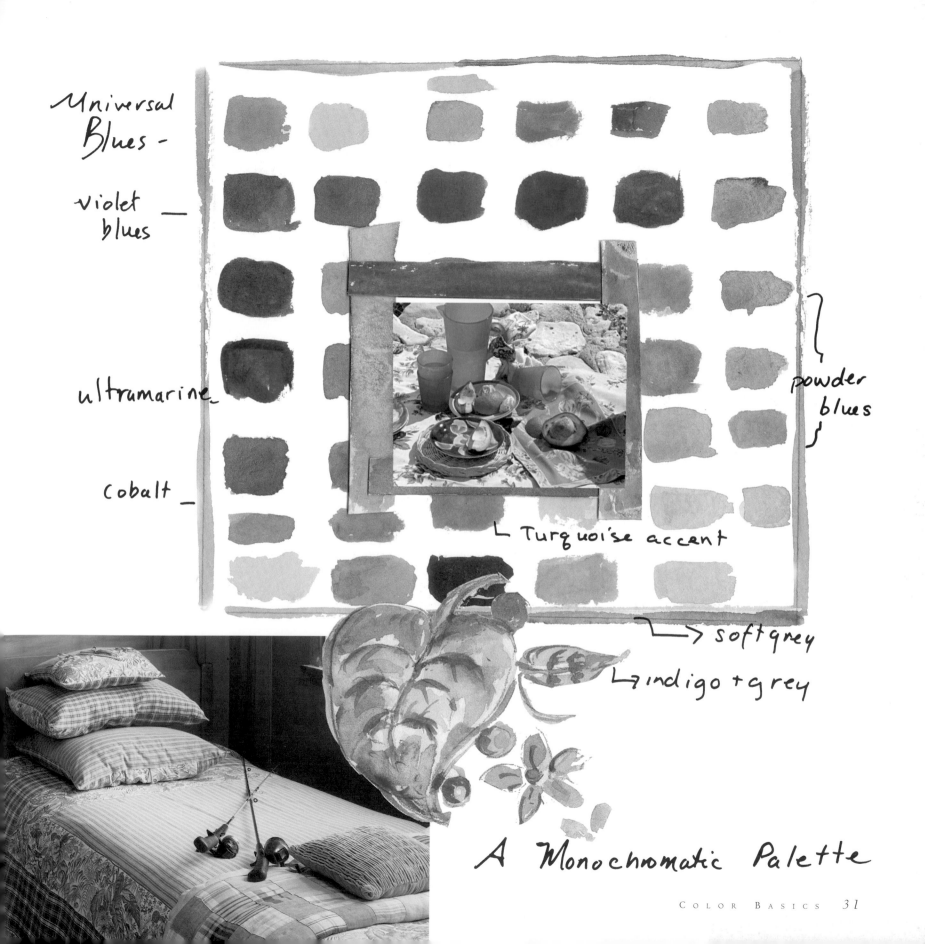

Universal
Blues –

violet
blues __

ultramarine __

cobalt __

powder
blues

∟ Turquoise accent

⤷ soft grey

∟ indigo + grey

A Monochromatic Palette

Nature Wheel
for
Tropical
Colors

bougainvillea

array of greens

sharp
yellow/
green

— shadow

— Red

— pinks

paint
to Match
blossom

fabric
reflects
colors
of
bougainvillea

olive —

Sand ↓   Soft   L gold
                gold

*I found a wonderful
palette in a favorite bush
of the tropical garden —
a bougainvillea.*

Practice by looking at things in nature. What is the accent? What pulls it together?

I found a wonderful palette in a favorite bush of the tropical garden—a bougainvillea. This hearty plant can be grown as a bush or a hedge, yet it is often seen spilling over walls in a cascade of color with sharp green leaves and pink, red, orange, white and magenta flowers. A lush growth of bougainvillea will elicit an "Oh, look at that!"response. Bougainvillea is a wonderful source of color in hot dry climates. It requires little water and a lot of sun.

With bougainvillea as my inspiration, the colors in the fabric of the cushions and tablemats convey the pink, green, golds and fuchsias. They all echo the bougainvillea clippings I gave to the painter. With four different bougainvillea petals and cuttings of green leaves, he was able to create the colors and paint four Adirondack chairs and a bench to reflect the splendid tropical hues. The painter managed to mix all the colors while the flowers were still fresh, and the chairs mirror nature beautifully.

ABOVE: *Colored wooden furniture mimics vivid tropical flowers.*

In the same setting, a fresh pineapple and some loitering coconuts complete the table of tropical color. Both the coconuts and the pineapple reaffirm the natural references of the color scheme and the setting. They actually add to the outdoor décor. Think about this when you are decorating for an event. A bushel of apples, a coconut, a pineapple and, of course, flowers, all are great decorating accents that add the color you need but also give geographical and seasonal meaning to the setting.

MORE ON COLOR

Color is a friend—an intimate, personal, close friend. Color forms our lives and frames our memories. Do you have a favorite color? Do you remember a dress you loved or a sunny day that glowed with yellow? Do you ever look at the color of your own skin, check out your hair or inspect your eyes?

Colors can feel drenched, deep and rich; or light, soft and powdery.

OPPOSITE PAGE: *Outdoor color needs to be bold to counteract the vastness and brightness of the outside.*

Mixing and Matching

When I talk about a color—for example, the universally popular color blue—I usually have in mind a particular blue, probably a midrange cobalt blue. But if you want to decorate in a blue palette, you will likely need more than a single color to accomplish this.

I like to mix different blues together. Lighter and darker tones of the same color can create layers of interest. Colors can feel drenched, deep and rich; or light, soft and powdery. A dark color may be used as an accent color on a vase, dishes or cushions, or conversely as a background color, perhaps for the sofa with accents of lighter shades on top. Look at one of my prints and see the dissection of a palette from a print to creativity, and how an entire decorating scheme can be achieved. Fabrics can combine in checks, prints and solids to achieve this layering color effect.

We are ourselves color—a palette of our own unique balance of light and dark tones and shades.

Is your skin softly freckled with a merge of peach and brown and vein blue? Or is it warm and brown and golden? Is it a pale-tinted pink, lighter on the palm than on the tips of your hand? Are the tones of your body rosy or olive? Are your lips light and pale or stained the color of berries? Do your eyes merge with your face? Are they blue eyes like forget-me-nots or are they brown as the very earth? We are, ourselves, color—a palette of our own unique balance of light and dark tones and shades.

You already live in a world of color and have all the ingredients within yourself and your world to understand color and enliven your home with colors that appeal to and complement you.

I want you to embrace color, open up to it and recognize how thoroughly color enters every moment of our lives.

LEFT: *Have you admired a friend's hair—chestnut glowing or golden curls, thick and dark, or fair wisps? Around us, around you, around me is a world of color.*
OPPOSITE PAGE: *Color clothing doesn't need to be relegated to a closet, it can accessorize a room.*

USING CONTRAST

An effective tool for creating dynamic color is utilizing contrast. A neutral background can be an effective backdrop for dramatic color. Stepping back to an environment where this is startlingly evident is in the harsh desert countries of the world, such as in the Rajasthan desert of India or the tree-bare landscape of Afghanistan, where naught but sand and sky can be seen in the landscape. The nomadic people have a vivid and compelling use of color.

When first traveling to the Far East some 30 years ago, my husband Chris and I were struck by the richness of dress in the dullest of landscapes. It seemed the barer the background nature had to offer, the more people fought to insinuate color into their lives. Persian carpets appear in tents in a desert. Camels are draped with gaudy decorative headgear, and saddlebags are finely woven with reds and oranges, browns and blacks. Nomadic women wear large silver anklets and gaily patterned skirts in Rajasthan and their Afghani cousins wear twirling dresses of Russian chintzes.

An American example of vivid color is found in New Mexico where cerulean blue door frames contrast against the soft brown adobe walls and cascades of hanging red chilies decorate the outside of homes. Patterned carpets and iron lanterns creating pools of light dispel the high-desert browns and taupes. It is no accident that Santa Fe and New Mexico are artistic centers in the United States. In such a modestly colored environment, art is needed.

Like spice to a meal, color adds zest to an environment.

OPPOSITE PAGE: *Color can be carried throughout a room in many ways including bright lines, accents of furniture and even stained-glass windows.*

It is as if our spirits call to color and color calls to us. Where color is lacking, people create it. Sometimes we get so out of touch with our basic human needs that we forget the essentials; and color is no exception.

Like spice to a meal, color adds zest to an environment. It can add the tart of a lemon or the piquancy of peppers; it is the cumin, paprika and cinnamon of our décor. A room or life without color is like a meal without spice—bland and medicinal. And a wonderful thing about the added "salt" of color to your décor is that calories don't exist!

Think of your own home and think of you. Is your home a desert in need of flowers? Is your home a landscape of neutrality, an unexplored opportunity for fun and style? Start adding color as a contrast to your environment. You may find that your neutral setting can take on many moods.

Are your rooms like a beige lady in need of a bright scarf? Is your home your own little desert of sand in need of an oasis?

Happy Accident

GLORIOUS
FADED GLORY

Remember that the strong sun will fade the brightest colors, so start bolder and plan on replacing outdoor sun-exposed items regularly. Sun-faded fabrics can be enjoyed as a distressed look, especially when coupled with woods. I like to use sun-faded blankets and cloths for picnics.

OPPOSITE PAGE: *While you may prefer a neutral white-on-white backdrop, see how soft gold and deep garnet reds bring life to the table.*

Let color in and she will show you her riches. Just as a bright lipstick, a shawl and pretty earrings can open a wardrobe to beauty, colorful fabrics, walls and accessories can do the same for your surroundings. If you have always been that beige lady, you will delight in the response that people will have as you open up to color.

In the same way a new dress gives a spring to your step, a vibrant tablecloth brings life to a kitchen table, a colorful quilt warms a room and the bright colors in a guest room say welcome without words. The first step to living with color is simply that—the first step.

I have a theory that beauty calls to beauty, that beauty longs for beauty, and that beauty attracts beauty and invites beauty. You can create an atmosphere that welcomes beauty. Once it enters your home, it will only grow. It is a transforming process; it is bigger than us. When you purchase your first beautifully colorful item, it will soon call for another and in time, you will have a home that resonates with your taste for beauty and color.

Nature Wheel for
Soft Coastal Color

green
cupboard

wall

flooring 2

add
stripe

flowers of
quilt

Straw   Sage   Smoke   soft aqua

Like good books that become good friends, each addition of color, each selection of a shapely vase and each framing of a child's artwork will be a declaration of your appreciation for life. The building of the journal of your home along with these colors and objects form a supportive friendship—they are a reflection of your individual taste.

Do you have children? I do; I have three sons. When we had our first boy, Cameron, we were so in love. We took our little pal everywhere. It was hard to imagine that if we ever had another child there would be enough love for him. We had our second boy, Lee, and our love grew bigger and wider and flowed right over to the big brother. So, he too experienced a new love in his life. And again, we learned that love—like color—knows no bounds when our third son, Kelly, joined the family.

Do not be afraid of adding color into your life; like the first son and then the second and third, there is always room. I might say that adding color is a good deal more risk-free than adding children!

In a Nutshell

- *Think of a color memory.*
- *Choose a color you love and build on it.*
- *Use bold colors outdoors.*
- *Add flowers and fruit for color accents.*
- *Use contrast to create dynamic moods with color.*
- *Spice it up!*
- *Add colorful cushions, a tablecloth or a shawl on a chair.*
- *Upgrade what you hang on books to create color accents in a room.*
- *Stand back, look, assess and ponder.*

Chapter Three

Defining Your Personal Colors

NATURE DOESN'T MATCH;
IT COORDINATES

If you see, like I do, nature as a source of all color, then you also see that nature doesn't match. Nature's colors vary but they still belong together. She is the perfect co-ordinator and a hapless matcher.

Have you ever worn a matching two-piece outfit and had somebody say to you, "Oh, that is a nice match!" Of course you haven't. They may say, "What a nice match" when the blue of your blouse picks up the blue flowers in your yellow skirt, but matching shades exactly is a thankless exercise. There is no goal other than matching, and there is no reward in the achievement of it. Mostly there is probably a lot of irritation in the accomplishment.

OPPOSITE PAGE: *This table setting is an oasis of rich, warm rusts and ivories against the intense greens of the surrounding forest. The buttercup yellow tea set provides vivid highlights of color.*

RIGHT: *Even though the same colors as the forest palette are used in the softer tones on this sofa, there is still strong contrast between the pinks and corals and the yellow.*

To enjoy color, you will need to let go of the perfect match.

To enjoy color, you will need to let go of the perfect match.

I have often used a phrase when referring to my prints, which all begin as hand-painted artworks: Not perfect, just perfectly beautiful. Let the beauty create the perfection.

In essence, this is the way I start my design season. I begin by painting. But that is simply artwork. Artworks come in many colors. So, simultaneously, as artworks are being developed, I put my color palettes together. I use a school notebook and begin assembling fabrics. I use one of my favorite fabrics on the cover as the collection evolves.

Most color stories start with a central print and build out from there, but sometimes I start with a favorite element and build up.

Cover a Book with Color

An easy way to play with color is to start on a small project such as covering a book. With a collection of calicos, plaids, ribbons and buttons, you can cover a journal or notebook with some of your favorite fabrics. Napkins make good book covers and you can get a wide array of fabrics to choose from and coordinate with.

Inside, you can start putting together your own favorite combinations—blues you like, for example, or corals or olives. Collect similar colors and separate them into chapters.

Limit the book to color palettes. Put your decorating ideas in another journal with a different cover. This way, when you are ready to decorate or shop, you can choose from your own fabric color palettes for your textile and paint choices. What a great tool! This is your own book of your favorite colors.

Most color stories start with a central print and build out from there.

OPPOSITE PAGE: *Staying in a palette of a color, like blues, can still be very exciting. Use different patterns and textures to provide variety.*

It could be a piece of embroidery to which I add a small check in the same colors, then a polka dot, then a floral. I often recolor two or three prints, using some of the embroidery colors and adding a few new colors to expand the usage. At the same time, I am thinking of curtains and add a few cuttings of velvet that might be for window coverings or solid cushions, or perhaps they'll be used as trims.

In this way, I build every collection so there is completeness to it from minor to major elements. This can be reinterpreted by using more or less of a palette or by mixing the fabrics with reverse emphasis—large print versus small print dominating, or playing up a solid or a check instead of a print. Of course, when these collections are complete, personal items may be added to the end result. Old laces or crisp eyelets can fit into many collections.

Let's look at this cycle from start to finish:

USING MULTICOLORS

A multicolored palette is certainly more challenging than a monochromatic one. Like any eclectic home, it takes more than two different elements to carry this off. I think of multicolor as three main color elements. In a print I would describe it as two sets of three colors in the same hue and one set of two colors in the same hue.

To visualize this, think of a pink rose and a yellow rose and green leaves. I would use

> *A multicolored palette is certainly more challenging than a monochromatic one.*

OPPOSITE PAGE: *You have to take time to absorb color, and mental relaxation actually stimulates creativity. Start with a book, and sleep away an afternoon.*
RIGHT: *Embroidery and crafts are also a great massage for the mind.*

ABOVE: *A mix of stripes, florals, pleated and crocheted cushions on a hand-stitched quilt gives real vintage charm to a country bedroom. The old botanical prints are ready for hanging.*

OPPOSITE PAGE: *Whether it's a mellow breakfast in bed or a snappy lunch with friends, I use color to help create the mood of my home.*

three yellows for the yellow rose (lighter and darker, maybe the darkest yellow is a gold and the lightest is a cream; the dominant color a mid yellow) and three pinks for the pink rose. My darkest pink may be almost red and my lightest could be a baby pink, the medium pink would be the dominant color and the light and dark colors are the accents. Conversely, a light color can dominate for a little more unusual look.

My green leaves would have two greens, a lighter and a darker green for shading. Through overlapping color, I can also achieve an olive brown by overlaying the red on green.

The background color will provide another strong element that can completely reinvent the color story. Imagine the scale between black and ecru for backgrounds, and all the colors in between. Changing a background color while maintaining the same "top" colors is a way to maintain harmony while adding change and contrast.

If I use this same basic palette in a smaller coordinating print, I could add a check or a stripe in a couple of these colors, a few

Mellow
Palette

main colors have equal depth

curtains

soothing color

accent

accent

*One of
the colors,
perhaps
the lighter
or medium
colors, could
be used
to paint
the walls.*

solids for cushions or curtains, perhaps in some of the more minor colors of the print. I am well on my way to having a lively multi-colored look that is still "under control" because the palette is all drawn from the original eight colors. Lighter and darker shades can, of course, be added.

One of the colors, perhaps the lighter or medium colors, could be used to paint the walls. A carpet could be a single color or you can try a carpet that incorporates just a few of the colors. Lamp shades, artwork and vases can all use these colors as a starting point. Metals such as silver, brass, pewter and copper each fit a little better with different palettes. Choose the one that works best with your colors for candlesticks, lamp bases and photo frames.

Multihued rooms can range from pastels to primaries and to rich wines and olives, so choose shades within the palette you want— be it soft or mid tones or dark and luxurious— then work this proportion formula into it.

OPPOSITE PAGE: *This bedroom is so natural a hibiscus poked its way in the door. Both green walls and the yellow cabinets and bed frame create the perfect canvas for the soft blue and white palette on the bed.*
ABOVE: *Color may be brought into a room in many ways, including a lamp shade, accessories and flowers from the garden.*

In a Nutshell

SIMPLE STEPS FOR MAKING YOUR PALETTE

• *Choose three colors in the same family. For example, three tones of red. Add three colors in a coordinating family, in this case three yellow shades, then add two to three greens as accents. Now you have a color palette to decorate with.*

• *You can use these colors all together in a print or in smaller amounts in checks, stripes, polka dots and solids.*

They all work together because they are from the same palette. The solid reds and blues can be used as background colors, furniture colors, etc.

• *Think of two flowers shaded in tints of red and tints of yellow, with green leaves, in a blue vase. The same formula can work with any combination of colors.*

OPPOSITE PAGE: *Bold beautiful colors make this front-porch setting enough to make any passerby stop and marvel at its impact.*

■ ■ ■

Chapter Four

Using Color
to Create
Mood

Check your memory file for an experience and understand the color connection.

I am naturally drawn to vibrant colors. I love butter yellows and periwinkle blues, olive greens and fresh corals. These colors are on the softer side of the primary colors— red, blue, yellow—from which all other colors are derived.

I love bright colors. To me, they are symbolic of joy. Color provokes emotion. It creates and asks for an emotional response. If we did not experience a response to color, there would be no need to create a look; all looks would be equal. Color gives value.

The response to color is subjective, it is personal and emotional. Yes, there are tried-and-true recipes, but these color recipes are based on historical response that continually elicits common feelings. This response, this visual understanding, says these colors affect me, they make me feel good or they make me feel happy or sad. Think of a gloomy room where your spirit quickly sinks, or a cold, barren, concrete place where feelings of anxiety are stimulated.

Color is all about our human ability to distinguish value; to see light and dark tones, shades and hues; and then to connect these colors to our own experiences. Check your memory file for an experience and understand the color connection.

I've already asked you to look back and ponder favorite colors from your past. Now I am asking you to thoughtfully ponder the emotion those colors evoke. Recall a summer day when the sun was warm and yellow, the grasses long and green. See them blowing; the sky is peaceful and vast in its blueness. Since childhood, you have seen these colors combined and they are embedded in your memory. Imitating this palette will elicit a response such as: What sunny colors! Or, how refreshing!

Color is wrapped up in memories and stirs response. So, in short, decorating with color is all about eliciting response, and creating an ambience. Like its cousin music, color calls out moods and attitudes. Prepare for the best!

In these days when Bach, Beethoven and other music greats can be heard in any home, so too can color—once the provenance of the affluent—be enjoyed in every room.

With paint and textiles, shade and light, you can aim as high as the masters in putting color together. A penchant for color opens

Colorful Concept

The animal and avian kingdom use color to conceal, attract and repel. It is our good fortune that we can use color to attract, comfort, nurture, calm and stimulate.

a vast world of visual pleasure. It is a tool, once unboxed, you will keep using for all your days.

FASHION-FORWARD COLOR

For many years, we have looked to the color trends in apparel to influence color in the home. In recent years, apparel and housewares have been competing style influences. On a trip to Paris, haunting the streets of Ste. Germaine for French inspiration with my friend Hélène (enjoying a pastry every hour or so), we stopped by a little shop that was a delightful cubby of a space spilling over with interesting and eclectic clothing.

We struck up a conversation with the owner, discussing trends and style. She was a chic young woman with a bohemian flair, who said she was getting her influences and picking up trends from the housewares industry. "They are at least two years ahead of the clothing designers," she said.

Without a doubt, there is much overlap between the two sectors. Rich apparel fabrics and delicate tailoring details have entered our homes through cushions and cloths,

When designing table and bed linens, I have always treated them as fashion.

quilts and carpets. It is a ripe time to experiment in decorating. The idea of using apparel as decorating touches in your décor is an opportunity to experiment with color ideas before making big purchases.

When designing table and bed linens, I have always treated them as fashion. I mine the influences of the clothing industry for all its rich details and change prints and colors seasonally.

Keeping in mind that people do not make over their homes as frequently as their wardrobes, "classic" color recipes add new accents every season. This is a great way to make sure that things continue to work together while still remaining fresh—stick to a palette and add.

A blue-and-white kitchen will always welcome another piece of blue pottery, or new curtains and table linens in the same palettes. I find that mixing napkins in similar shades is a fun way to keep a table fresh and at the same time, hang on to old favorites while incorporating newness. In the same blue-and-white kitchen, your table could have

a range of napkins from light to dark blues, from prints to blue-and-white gingham, from white lace to jacquards, while still feeling unified by a common color.

ADDING INSTANT MOOD COLOR

Flowers and greens can bring instant mood and color to a setting. When you peruse a good decorating magazine, there are always beautiful flowers. It's not an accident; the professionals know the effect flowers have on décor. Think of flowers as the highlight of your color scheme. Add them as a reinforcing color element by trying blue bachelor buttons on a blue table or adding a bouquet in contrast as a frisson of color—pink coneflowers would be delightful with blue. Or try a complementary yellow coreopsis with sharp green leaves. These ideas give height and color to your setting; they also bring nature indoors and create a mood from elegant to casual.

Think of flowers as the highlight of your color scheme.

OPPOSITE PAGE: *This is a classic blue-and-white kitchen, with yellow accents in food, a pitcher and flatware. Mix and match old and new blue-and-white elements to keep the décor lively and new.*

Quick Flower Arranging Tips

The general rule of thumb for flowers is two-thirds in the vase and one-third out. This gives a good proportion so the flowers do not look lopsided. You don't need to have flower arrangements professionally done. Long grasses, palm fronds, garden flowers, pine boughs and tropical sea grape as well as supermarket bouquets can all make dynamic arrangements. Don't overfuss with your arrangements; stand back and see if you have achieved the desired impact. If you haven't, you may want to pop in a few more accents such as artificial flowers.

Colorful Concept

COLOR AT THE READY

I like to keep a basket of assorted napkins in the same palette handy so that whatever napkin is chosen it will automatically coordinate. (No last-minute decision making here.) Mixing different textures in the same colors is a powerful way to give depth and interest to décor without introducing new colors.

A collection of vases is as handy as a selection of napkins. Different sizes will fit different needs. A low vase next to a side table or atop a library shelf can be delightful, while tall vases command center stage in a buffet. Glass vases show green stems well, while colored or metal vases give an additional color boost to a setting.

A plate rail is an excellent spot for vases and platters. If you have space in your kitchen or dining room, I suggest adding one. With a bit of molding, you have a whole new place for display.

ABOVE: *A plate rail can be an uplifting display for your dish and vase collections.*

Nature Wheel Wild Rose Palette

Stripes

Wall

yellow accents ↳

—biscuit

florals

leaves and accents

furniture →

LEFT: *A collection as simple as hand-painted boxes can inspire a color palette.*

floor ← tile

HOW TO *Fold a Napkin Shoe*

Begin with a 24" x 24" napkin, face down.

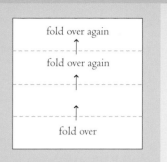

STEP 1: Fold the bottom quarter up to the center along the horizontal. Fold up this portion again at the centerline and then again to form a long rectangle.

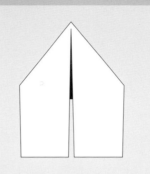

STEP 2: Place index finger at the top-center edge of the rectangle. Fold in the top left and right corners along the diagonal so that the edges meet perpendicularly at the center. (The napkin should look like a house.)

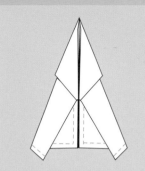

STEP 3: Keeping your index finger in the same place, fold in the top left and right corners once again along the diagonal so that the edges meet in the center.

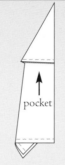

STEP 4: Fold the right half onto the left half along the centerline. Notice the pocket.

STEP 5: Take the left-hand corner of the bottom flap and fold it to the right along the diagonal.

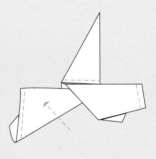

STEP 6: From the right-hand bottom corner, fold the bottom flap directly to the left so that the top edge of the flap meets the bottom edge of the pocket.

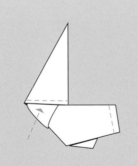

STEP 7: Take the left-hand flap and tuck it snugly into the pocket.

STEP 8: Turn it over and stand it up so that the point is facing you and fold the top flap down and around the shoe to look like a cuff.

Now you have a perfect little shoe to fill with little surprises.

CREATING COLOR ENVIRONMENT

Color influences your environment; it adds the elusive concept of feeling. Feelings are hard to describe, analyze or dissemble, but we know them when we feel them!

Without feelings, decorating wouldn't exist.

Again, go back into your memory and think of a room where you felt good. What is your memory of it?

It's bohemian, different; I was intrigued.

It's masculine and strong.

OPPOSITE PAGE: *It's calming, peaceful and thoughtful.*

PASTEL PALETTES

For an innocent and delicate feel, for a very special event like a wedding picnic or garden party, try using soft pastels. Mint green, baby pink and lavender with a strong grounding of white are as delicate and whimsical as a bride's bouquet. For a wedding picnic setting, I have used white crochet and lace as foundation builders and added a host of pastel pillows for the romantic couple. The silver of a candelabrum and champagne bucket sits well against pastels and adds elegance and humor to the outdoor picnic. Unexpected touches, such as a candelabrum outdoors, are the unique features that keep a setting from becoming formulaic.

It is easy to cover a small "vow" book with an organdy napkin. It's enough to make the young woman pop the answer (I do!) rather than wait for the question to be asked.

OPPOSITE PAGE: *Put magic into a bridal shower by creating a feminine picnic. Velvets, organdies and white lace can all be part of the keepsake for the bride's trousseau.*

A delicate pastel palette can be used in a young girl's room or a nursery. I would use it reluctantly in a master bedroom or a public space; it is too feminine and limiting.

WARM VIBRANT PALETTES

Colors known to give warmth can be found in the yellow and red families and include corals, yellows, golds, oranges, pinks and peaches. In my tropical living room you find these sunny colors. I've added sharp olive accents to give a lively mood. Red lacquer Chinese benches and side tables are an unlikely but fitting choice for the tables.

This is an interesting example of how moving your furniture around until it finds the right space can work. The benches and side tables were originally in a small guest bedroom. They are attractive pieces of furniture, but they did not contribute anything to the room. Placed next to colorful couches and chairs in the right place, they come alive and pull together the room. Color helps unify décor.

It's enough to make the young woman pop the answer (I do!).

CLOSET COLOR

Consider this easy and inexpensive way to add a final touch of color to a room: Check your closets. A favorite jacket, hat, sweater or shawl may add the splash of color you need. Whether hung on a hook, laid over the back of a couch or thrown over a banister, these accents may enliven a space as effectively as your most carefully researched purchase. A practical person may say, "What is the difference between clothes hanging around and a mess?" Well, the difference is that you have chosen what is on the back of the chair, and it is one of your favorite things.

The yellows in this family room are warm yellows with a touch of red. They are not the tart yellow of a lemon, but the creamy yellow of butter. As my husband has asked, "It's all about food, isn't it?"

TROPICAL COLORS

Use vivid color to get a tropical feel. Strong pinks and greens feel tropical, as do cerulean blues and bright yellows. Tropical color is often used outdoors or in a room that opens to the outdoors. You can be bolder and brighter with your color choice when incorporating the outdoors.

Tropical color is synonymous with fun and holiday; be playful with your accessories, use things like fish cushions, lanterns and trays.

MASCULINE MATTERS TOO

I think of masculine color as dark, rich and earthy. I use plenty of woven fabrics to create a masculine look (plaids and stripes) and less flowered fabrics. I use earthy reds, wines and olives with dark wood furniture

OPPOSITE PAGE: *The family room in my tropical home is warmed with soft colors in the yellow and red families.*

with strong lines. Use more dark solids and less fine detailing. Be bolder and simpler with your choice of fabrics. Bookcases can look good in a masculine room as well as trunks, leather armchairs and wooden stools.

A library or den takes on dark colors like these well. Mix objects between books to keep the display interesting; brass and copper objects and photos in leather frames feel "masculine."

A room that feels masculine should be rich in color, strong in traditional style and genuine. No flimsy materials or lightweight chairs here. It should feel made to last, and heartening as a consequence.

OPPOSITE PAGE: *The warm wood walls of this bedroom are complemented by the colors in the patchwork velvet spread, giving the room a masculine feel.*

In a Nutshell

■   ■   ■   ■

- *Use plate rails to raise color up the wall.*

- *Use a collection of vases to add spots of color.*

- *Yellows are vibrant and warm colors.*

- *Masculine rooms have strong bones; wood, leather, rich color contribute to this.*

- *Think of the mood you want in a room.*

- *Tropical color combines well with outdoor environments. Go bright.*

- *Blues are soothing and cool.*

Chapter Five

Working Color into Your Life

ABOUT PAINT

I have a predisposition for colored walls. Between a white wall and a painted wall, I will always choose color. I use medium-tone paint colors—not too light nor too dark. These colors anchor a strong color story and add tremendous value to a room. I believe that people look better in a colored room. Their complexions are warmed by color; just as soft lighting gives a glow, so will corals, pinks and earth-toned walls give a glow.

I generally keep ceilings white or ivory, avoiding blue-white, which can be harsh. Use a white with a hint of yellow or pink. For baseboards, moldings, doors and most woodwork, I use white or ivory. If there is a good amount of woodwork, plate rails or double-crown moldings, I may introduce a second shade of the wall color (coral and terra-cotta, for example).

OPPOSITE PAGE: *This is a quintessential family table with an old-fashioned and unusual tablecloth, and is even more alive because of the paint color used on the walls and cabinet.*
RIGHT: *An adult-size chair cushion is just the right size colorful padding for a high chair.*

Natural woodwork can be left as is, or stained a richer or redder color to give it life. Red-toned woodwork is my favorite. Again, it goes with a lot and warms a room. In our lake house, the walls are paneled in wood, as are many of the ceilings. We painted the ceilings, doors and windows a bright white to offset the dark wood. This keeps the home from looking too dark, and gives life to the interiors.

We have a coffered ceiling in the dining room of our Vermont home that we lived with "au natural" for two years before daring to paint it white. I felt so guilty painting all that natural dark wood, but the coffered ceiling had started to feel like a coffin and it had to go. With the ceiling painted white, the whole room opened up and became more upbeat. Major changes like this can take time and decisions in painting natural wood are permanent, so think carefully and find a way to ease into the change. In our case, we painted the doors first, before touching the ceilings.

If you have painted your wall and it doesn't look good, you can always use your painted color as your first coat and another hue for your second coat.

On the opposite page are eight palettes I find effective and reliable.

It is easy to make a mistake with paint. Though easy to correct, many people will paint a whole room and live with it rather than repaint, so here are some reliable colors that work well together.

Notice that the yellows are buttery, not lemony and the whites and ivories are creamy, not blue. The "biscuit" is warm, with red not yellow. If you go too light in your wall color, you will not get the impact of that vast canvas; you will get a wall that dirties easily and gives a weak contribution to the room.

Difficult colors like pinks can be sponged on top of each other along with cream to create a color that glows but is indefinable.

In general, I don't use blue on walls because it is difficult to match and tends to have a cooling effect rather than a warm one. I love blue, but I would rather use the hue on elements in the room.

Palette 1

Coral

Terra-cotta

Ivory

Palette 2

Apple Green

Yellow

Ivory Rose

Palette 3

Soft Yellow

Ivory

Sunflower

Palette 4

Rose

Soft Rose

Soft Pink

Palette 5

Sage

Cream

Palette 6

Terra-cotta

Ivory Rose

Palette 7

Warm Biscuit

Warm White

Sponging Combination

Bisque

Blush

Melon

SPONGING TECHNIQUE:

Begin by painting a base coat of bisque on the walls. Then sponge a layer of blush on top, finishing with a sponged layer of melon.

If you want to choose your own paint colors, I suggest buying the smallest amount of paint possible and painting a portion of the wall to be sure you like the color. If you have painted your wall and it doesn't look good, you can always use your painted color as your first coat and another hue for your second coat. For example, if your yellow is too sharp and lemony, try painting over it with a warmer, more buttery yellow.

Is the coral more orange than you wanted? Use a browner terra-cotta color on top to tone it down.

I had this experience in a kitchen where the cabinets were to be painted a rosy coral color. When the cabinets arrived painted, the effect was overwhelmingly pink—too pink for a kitchen. I repainted the cabinet doors a darker terra-cotta and the pink was balanced. The kitchen ended up having an Arts & Crafts feel and the two-toned cabinets played against the two-toned tile floor. Serendipity—take advantage of it. Mistakes can take you in new directions; follow the excitement.

Serendipity— take advantage of it. Mistakes can take you in new directions; follow the excitement.

LIGHTING THE WAY

When you are thinking about painting be sure to keep lighting in mind. Fine ceiling fixtures, wall sconces and occasional lamps, all add mood and soften an environment beautifully—and they affect color. Avoid "pot lights," fluorescents and harsh overhead lights; they will steal your mood with the flip of a switch.

An overlit room will cause colors to look garish and antiseptic. Keep strong lighting for the daytime or for activities like reading, writing or computer work. These areas work best with task lighting such as desk lamps.

The pool of light they create makes the rest of the environment more interesting.

Undercounter lighting adds a soft glow in a nighttime kitchen, while accent lights highlight corners and alcoves. In India, niches are often built into homes to house statues of gods and are lit with oil lamps, which symbolize a light in the darkness for gods to find their way into a home. A warm light illuminating a cluster of family photos creates a miniature family "shrine" in your own home.

Lightbulbs with a yellow or red tint can add unexpected drama in a corner. A colored lightbulb can lend a bistro style to the area. Yellow light gives a golden glow and softens the complexion. Consider it in rooms where you want a warm ambience.

Different types of windows call for different coverings.

WINDOW COVERINGS AND COLOR

Different types of windows call for different coverings. Evaluate your needs before plunging in. Do you have an outdoor environment that extends the visual space of your room? Go easy on curtains here. Are your curtains for privacy, closing out the outside? If so, they will become a major investment and key element in a room. Do you want to block light, or allow light in? The degree of opacity will determine the style of your curtains. A lined curtain will be heavier and therefore less fabric will be required.

Sheer, organdy, voile and "tissue" fabrics create magical reflections with light. Avoid polyester substitutes; the light will not reflect off them the way it will with natural fabrics. The gold, silver or copper of the thread will twinkle and dance with the light of your window. A tissue fabric is a fine transparent fabric partially woven with a metallic thread. Tissues, originally the domain of the maharajahs, were woven with real gold or silver. Why shouldn't you enjoy the same luxurious look?

Window treatments and the light they provide or block out will enhance the colors of your room as much as your wall colors. They also are a source of natural lighting. Normally, unless they are leading the décor theme, curtains are added after your room has been painted. That way, it is easier to coordinate.

HANG IT UP!

A friend of mine lives in a big, drafty Victorian in Boston. "I use your quilts for curtains," she says. What a fabulous idea!

Quilts block the light beautifully, eliminate drafts and with the use of brass rings and clips, they are a cinch to install. A tieback can be fashioned out of a large napkin sewn on the bias and hooked to the window frame, or for a more bohemian look, consider using a beaded belt as a tieback.

Using a quilt as curtains also is a good way to rotate your favorite possessions off the bed (or out of storage) and onto the wall. Curtains provide major color in a room; they can lead the color direction and provide a unifying solid that pulls together diverse color elements.

HOW TO *Make a Curtain from a Quilt*

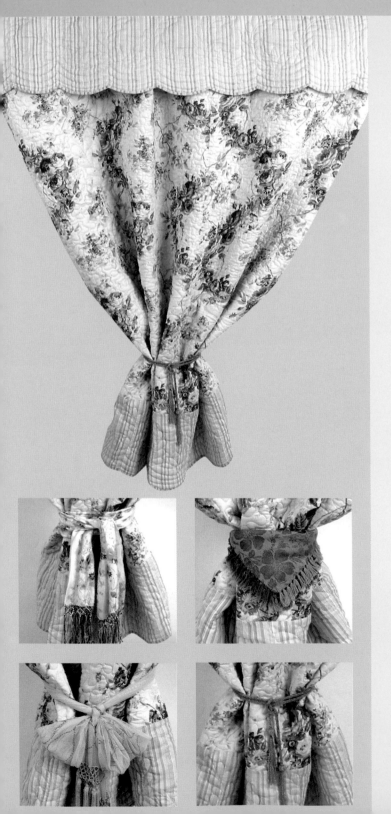

This will be one of the easiest projects you'll ever try!

Fold the top of your reversible quilt over towards the front of the quilt approximately 15". (This will be the side that will face into the room.) This now forms a valance.
If your quilt has a scalloped edge, then you will also have a scalloped valance. With heavy round brass clips, clip onto the top of the valance at 10" intervals. As your quilt will make a heavy curtain, you will need a strong brass or iron rod as well as strong brass or iron clips. That's it! As you have not stitched your curtain, this can easily be used again as a quilt.

If you want to make a permanent curtain out of your quilt make a 3" channel along the upper edge to put your rod through and dispense with using the brass rings. Hang like a normal rod curtain.

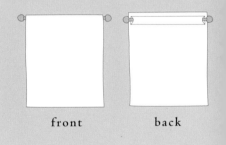

front   back

Tiebacks can pull the center showing the window on two sides, or to one side in a romantic sweep.

Another permanent solution would be to make a 3" channel along the upper edge on the front of your quilt for a more decorative look. This will also hang like a normal rod curtain.

front

A powerful floral print, a dramatic batik or a rich ethnic cloth can add great color and drama to a room.

FRAMED FABRIC

Add color with cloth. An inexpensive way to add just the right color to a room without investing in original art is to frame fabric. The fabric can be right out of your décor.

Pick out coordinating napkins of different sizes in similar palettes and create a montage of color. Similarly framed textiles, antique and otherwise, also are a way to preserve fragile textile art. A powerful floral print, a dramatic batik or a rich ethnic cloth can add great color and drama to a room. As textiles are relatively inexpensive, this is an easy way to dress the walls of a room. Think of a frame as an opportunity to put something on the wall; don't limit yourself to artwork.

More is more. A collection of textiles is more interesting than a single piece. In framing, I like to use wooden frames with a burnished gold finish, which matches everything. Having all of the frames in similar finishes helps coordinate diverse artwork.

Framed textiles typically do not require matting or glass. You'll want to pay tribute to those textile textures, particularly if they are embroidered or beaded, for which no glass is required. Textiles are light-sensitive so if you have something of collector's quality, you should be aware of sunlight or strong lamplight. Textiles eventually can become too fragile for daily use. Framing special pieces will keep them alive for future generations and give new value to them, as well as provide major color in a room.

A charming way to protect an especially valued piece is to create a small curtain that covers the piece from the strong light, and is then raised for viewing.

BEST OF SHOW

A letter from my childhood art teacher—a neighbor—recently inspired me to remember my girlhood, her influence on it, and to recapture an old idea. She sent me photos of a neighborhood art show she had put on for me and my friends when we were children. A photo brought back that proud summer day when we hung our winter's work on her fence and had family and friends admire it. She even called the local paper, and we were very proud. Her letter inspired me to have a mini art show with friends and family. Our own little art show, this time with elegant tables, bouquets of flowers and artists easels with paintings and drawings propped up on stone walls. What fun! Create your own 'vernissage' and live like an artist in your own backyard.

APPLY COLOR WITH ART

Art is a soul-filled way to bring color to a room. It doesn't just add color, but brings the mood the artist has created to the setting. If you have a new purchase, or you are an artist or belong to an art club, create your own mini vernissage. This small art show of sorts can be arranged and hung on a wall, and will bring more impact than simply pounding a nail and to suspend a single work by itself.

PARENTING YOUR DECOR

Did your parents ever say to you, "Those are the wrong friends; I don't want you hanging out with them?" Our childhoods are full of warnings, guidance and directions about choice. If you take that idea and extrapolate it to the choices in your home, you can ease a lot of problems. Simply said, get rid of unattractive disharmonious "stuff."

Add only items of value, richness and integrity. Value, richness and integrity don't mean expensive; these qualities come at all

OPPOSITE PAGE: *April (center) at a vernissage in Montreal, 1964.*

price points, as does poor quality and bad design. Because something is expensive, doesn't mean it's beautiful. Train your eye to see beauty in the commonplace, and create a home that is uncommonly beautiful. Make good choices.

BLENDING AND MIXING COLOR

The impact of color becomes greater the more shades that are used. To achieve a look that hums with color, you need to layer colors on top of each other. Extend your color palettes so that coral reaches up to oranges and reds, then leans back to golds and yellows. This will suffuse a room with color; you will feel the embrace of color and share a color "experience."

A honey-colored wooden cabinet will come alive with a bouquet of red flowers. Like radiant embers in a fireplace, red accents can make a room catch fire. Use red to ignite colors by using accent cushions, flowers, a throw or candles in red. Red has power and it fits in a number of color ranges. Strong pinks and wines are sophisticated substitutes-for red.

Remember to give color room to breathe.

Remember to give color room to breathe. When putting together palettes, you will want to give breathing room to the colors. Here are some points I think will help:

- *White breaks up blues*
- *Ivory softens browns*
- *Orange makes brown come alive*
- *Butter yellow calms corals*
- *Red brightens black*
- *Yellows contrast olives*
- *Ivories coordinate with sages*
- *Vibrant multicolored palettes need yellow*
- *Olive greens balance many colors*

Just standing back and looking at your colors will help you to know if you should continue to "layer" more colors in the same tones or add contrasting color.

OPPOSITE PAGE: *A herringbone texture such as this duvet provides pattern in a nonprint way. The headboard, covered with a cotton cloth, picks up the colors of the Haitian painting above the bed. Green palm leaves bring nature into the bedroom.*

SEASONAL COLOR

A common tune from people transported from other regions is: "I love it here, but I miss the change of seasons." What do they mean? A big part is that they miss the color changes of the year they are accustomed to. It may be from the blue-gray of winter to the green shoots and mounting beauty of spring; to the riot of summer color, when the pinks, yellows and blues compete with verdant hills and golden fields; or the apex of seasonal awe—the crowning glory of a breathtaking fall, when rusts, oranges, golds, crimson reds, falling leaves and pumpkin-littered fields beneath a changing sky are all aglow.

Even in climates where there are not dramatic seasonal changes, natives speak affectionately of the light changes of fall and the crisp clear tones of the summer colors by the ocean. This seasonal panorama of natural hues is the epitome of living with color.

With the abundance of colorful textiles and the mimicry of nature's rhythm, we can adopt these same colors in our homes.

Colorful Concepts

WHERE DID THE GREEN GO?

My paint box is always out of green. Green is not a central color in my paintings, yet I've concluded that green is used in almost all of my prints to some degree. I prefer olive-toned green (with hints of yellow) to forest greens (with hints of blue). Look at your room palette. Does it need a little green? A vase of green leaves, a green cushion or green curtains might be what's needed.

OPPOSITE PAGE: *The vivid colors of changing fall leaves are the inspiration for print, plaid and striped fabric designs.*

Autumn Palette

Gold, olives, rusts, red and orange—these hues are loved universally and can be treated in a masculine manner in a family room, kitchen, bedroom or den. This is a very flexible palette that can be used throughout the home by emphasizing a different color in each room.

Summer Palette

Pinks, sunny yellows, fuchsia, greens—this is a true "happy" palette that is ideal on a summer table, in a garden setting, in bedrooms and children's rooms.

The riot of color found in a June garden and the cacophony of bright blossoms is pure joy to the eye and to the spirit.

Spring Palette

Blues, yellows, periwinkles, greens—this is a true perennial palette as it features the favorite periwinkles of early hyacinths, the vibrant golds and reds of waving tulips and the greens of new grass, new buds and new life. These are vibrant colors for dining rooms, family rooms and bedrooms.

Winter Palette

Here I use rich colors to counteract nature's message of a sleeping world. I do not try to match the cool blues and soft grays of the winter sky; but I use the rich contrast of burgundies, purples and olives. This is a wonderful palette for living rooms, libraries, dens and art studios.

Chapter Six

Entertaining in Color

Quick Color

- *A shawl or pashmina also can serve as a tablecloth.*

- *Try using place mats or antimacassars as chair back covers.*

- *Cover unattractive storage with fabric. This can lend a hint of color to a room or outdoor area and disguise an unattractive box or crate.*

Once you have become comfortable with color and added its beauty to your home, it's likely you'll be in the mood to share it with family and friends. Don't let the joy of color stop with your décor; be sure to bring it into your entertaining too.

I have enjoyed entertaining in many different places and styles. My favorites are relaxed settings where more emphasis is placed on my guests and being able to enjoy each other, rather than big productions that keep me away from everyone. After all, I invited them so I could be with them, not to hide in the kitchen. I'd like to share some of my favorite entertaining stories with you.

OPPOSITE PAGE: *Vivid corals "pop" the green colors of this outdoor setting. The color of the flowers is so vivid, I can imagine a hummingbird nearby.*

A LITERARY LUNCHEON

A book club or group of friends with a passion for reading loves being invited to a lunch with literature as its theme. When I planned such a gathering, I set up around a roaring fire, and draped the chairs with shawls to ward off cold and to create the ambience of a late-nineteenth-century literary salon. A small candelabrum with shade was recovered with newsprint, napkin rings were made from newsprint and the centerpiece was a stack of books. If you don't have any old books, you can spray-paint books gold to give them a nice burnished antique look for your centerpiece. If you don't have anything suitable, try a secondhand bookstore. They are full of old books that are not all collectible.

The menu card was illustrated with simple watercolors, and listed different authors for the appetizer, main dish and dessert. Next to each place setting was a card to write

OPPOSITE PAGE: A book-themed luncheon is sure to please any avid reader. Keep the event comfortable and cozy by leaving a sweater or shawl on the back of each chair.

The menu card was illustrated with simple watercolors, and listed different authors for the appetizer, main dish and desert.

Inspired Uses

ALL BOOKED UP

- *Use books as a centerpiece.*

- *Make a menu card, naming every course for the writer's discussion.*

- *Make napkin rings from newspaper.*

- *Provide a note card with a paintbrush to 'draw' conclusions after discussion.*

- *Re-cover a candle shade with the page of a favorite book. Don't want to tear a book? Scan or copy it.*

Lake
Dominoes.
                    game 1   2   3   4
Joe   42   32
Robin   12   18
Eileen   0   24
Sarah   18   6
Mick   6   20

one's conclusions about the book being discussed— with a paintbrush!

A plaid cloth in autumn hues of rust, gold and olive served as the undercloth, with an embroidered tea cloth laid on top. The jacquard napkins in plaid colors joined a basket of burnt orange mums.

DOMINOES ON THE DOCK

This theme table makes spending an afternoon at the lake a delightful dalliance. You don't have to be by a lake to make this a wonderful afternoon; the right color palette can evoke a waterside afternoon.

Spend the morning finding ingredients in the grass and woods nearby. One great find on one of my walks was some sheets of birch bark that I decided to use as a tally card. What a fun way to keep track of scores, and it makes a wonderful keepsake to include in your journal to recall a summer day and the names of your guests. Be sure to date the card at the bottom. It's always fun to note the

OPPOSITE PAGE: *An afternoon of dominoes by the lake can be just as cheerful anywhere when you use linens in the colors of summer.*

Inspired Uses

A DAY OF GAMES

- *Have children collect birch bark (not from the tree, from the ground).*

- *Write invitations and tally cards on birch bark.*

- *Have children collect leaves, grasses, flowers, etc. for centerpieces.*

- *Use a gong, a bell or an echo to call people to events.*

weather, too (e.g. sunny and bright, July 25). This will help recall the date, and it is also fun to benchmark the day's weather against another year.

Long water iris leaves tied around green-and-blue napkins folded together make a natural napkin ring. A large ceramic pedestal bowl holds a colorful salad. Blue dishes and green glasses echo the colors of the cloths. A blue undercloth on the table, bursting with summer sunflowers, echoes the joys of the warm bright season. Blue picks up the color of the summer sky. Mixing plaids and prints in a summer setting reinforces the relaxed casual feel of the long days.

A BIRTHDAY CELEBRATION

When my mother-in-law celebrated her 80th birthday, the party warranted time and care to show our love and appreciation. I'm sure you feel the same about many members of your family.

Like most families, ours straddles many miles. We gathered all of the children, in-laws and friends from afar at our lake house, and stayed the weekend for the birthday bash.

I painted an invitation that included an itinerary of the weekend's events, with humorous sketches to emphasize the activities. If you are not very clever at sketching, you can cut out pictures from magazines, pop in photos or visit the web for some clip-art ideas. Once you assemble your invitation, color-copy one for each guest.

We sealed ours in an envelope that was closed with candle wax and an evergreen cutting. I also put one in each guestroom, with some blank paper and a pencil and instructions to note a special phrase about our celebrant on

OPPOSITE PAGE: *An invitation to a special gathering can be color-copied and embellished with watercolor or color pencil.*

Agenda on the occasion of
Mary Cornell's
80th Birthday. at Bark Lake
Boreal Forest.
Quebec

Aug 15 - meet and greet at Millers landing
Thurseve!! settle in cottage's 2 or 3.

Aug 16 - breakfast at Main house (#1)
Fri morn.   Golf at Arundel Golf Course.
8:30-10   (Senior males 16-81) Timings 10:56, 11:04
10am-   depart from cottage one at 10:00AM.
Golf   ladies & junior males - nature walk,
            water activities, peaceful pursuits
1pm - buffet lunch, at cottage 1.
4:00pm meet at Millers landing
6:30 cocktails and dinner at Alfred's.

Aug 17 - breakfast 9-11 at cottage !.
11   water activities all day.
    buffet lunch.
    Sea Plane Ride (weather permitting)
    Birthday bbq - cottage one.
    TTFN !   ch - 80!

a piece of paper. These expressions were strung along the fireplace and added laughter and silliness to the weekend.

My mother-in-law is an artist so gifts of colored pencils and paper were included for everyone. We bought half a dozen straw hats and had lots of photos taken of ladies posing in hats. Breakfast/brunch was the gathering meal every morning and the table overflowed with the joyous colors of summer fruits, siz-zling bacon, scones and eggs. Breakfast is a

ABOVE & LEFT: *Restful spots dappled in afternoon sunlight offer colorful places to rest and enjoy the day.*

great meal for the generations and at a family weekend, it is good to make the most of it.

QUIET PLACES FOR GUESTS

If you have weekend guests, surely you are not going to want to spend every minute together. You can make their visit memorable by providing a quiet place for them to relax and enjoy the setting of your home. Since the view from the porch at the lake house is so lovely, I was inspired to set a table for painting and journaling.

An outdoor setting requires bold color to stand up to the big landscape. I chose a quilt with a black background and many bright jewel colors. Chair cushions in prints that match the quilt make the outdoor space special. Get out the bedroom cushions and move them onto the verandah, where they can dress up the seating.

An old wooden panier (basket) was brought back to life when I painted pink flowers on the sides and covered the lid with a matching napkin. It held all the cards and envelopes I was working on.

Inspired Uses

Use a soft quilt as a tablecloth and layer it with a bolder coordinating print on top. This is a very European look that greatly extends the use of your bedding, and also accommodates a large-size table.

Inspired Uses

If you live in a warm climate, you have the opportunity to hang artwork outdoors. Here, the smoky blues on the blankets and cushions of the swing provide the missing color in this all-green landscape.

The painting makes an attractive outdoor piece of artwork and adds great beauty.

EVERYDAY VISITS

It may just be for a cup of tea, but even the briefest visit from a friend calls for a colorful setting. Dramatic contrast is the key to the success for a striking table setting.

A rich black tablecloth, printed with lively red apples, over a red cloth set against a yellow wall illustrates this perfectly. Flowers that match the colors of the table and the colors of the fruit emphasize the color palette. The yellow wall color balances the vivid colors on the table. White net curtains embroidered in dark red and green pick up the colors of the cloth and are another contrast to the boldness of the black. To avoid the table being too busy, choose a solid color napkin such as red. I even like taking a step further by serving food and drink that tie the scheme together like lemonade to match yellow walls.

OPPOSITE PAGE: *Apples of all colors dance around the tablecloth and on the table. The red tablecloth under the black one gives strong contrast. I like the way the delicate embroidered net curtains have the same vivid red and green colors of the apple cloth.*

In a Nutshell

■ ■ ■

AMBIENCE

Color can lose all of its appeal if the ambience isn't right, especially when you entertain. In the hope of helping set an enjoyable and pleasant mood for your party, I offer these tips:

- *Be generous. Even if you are serving hot dogs, have plenty. If it's boeuf bourguignon, assume it will be so delicious that your guests will want seconds. Don't leave your guests counting the shrimp to know if they can have one.*

- *Offer a drink as soon as people enter, and have two or three different choices. This truly is an ice breaker.*

- *Have a bartender or make your bar accessible so people feel comfortable helping themselves.*

- *Like musical chairs, have a few chairs short of the crowd so people will stand up and mix.*

- *Are children invited to the party? Let them pass around snacks.*

- *Don't be like some people and put everything away for a party, Guests enjoy looking at other people's stuff. This "stuff" can also be great conversation starters.*

- *Never tell your guests what to do. Some hosts spend more time admiring their guest's boots and assigning spaces for their coats than actually talking to their guests. Keep it easy—coats upstairs; boots over here.*

- *Clean up later. There's nothing worse than a host who is not there.*

OPPOSITE PAGE & RIGHT: *The winter holidays are always more cheerful when vibrant colors are used to decorate for the season.*

More Nuts

- Make all your efforts before people arrive and then let the evening take over. If it is a big party, a crowd that is a little too big for the space creates more fun than a room that is too big for the crowd. People love to jostle and bump into each other and get caught up in someone else's conversation; it makes them feel like they're in the right place—it is so crowded!

- Don't forget candles. You may want to put these great mood setters high up or on out-of-the-way tables so fire is not an issue.

- Warm things up. A fire in a fireplace is always a nice touch.

- Turn on the music. A little background music can be welcoming, especially at the beginning and end of the evening. Control the volume so your guests can hear each other.

- Turn off the overhead lights. Nobody wants to have their pores inspected; evenings are about soft lighting.

- Stock up your bathrooms. Don't forget the extra towels and emergency amenities. Include flowers or a tea light in the bathroom.

- Don't fuss over spills. The person is already embarrassed enough—wipe and move on. Actually, it's better if someone else wipes up, your guest will feel worse if the hostess is doing it.

- Say goodbye. When some guests leave early, it can be a real downer on a party—suddenly there's an exodus! Don't dally over these goodbyes; a gentle wave can suffice. Carry on with those who are there. You will catch up with the early leavers another time.

- Keep the refrigerator current. Lots of parties gravitate to the kitchen, so update your fridge with photos, quips or ideas that people might enjoy seeing or reading.

- Are children at home or have they been invited to the party? If it's an adult party, hire a babysitter to get the kids to bed after they have played with the other children and enjoyed their own special treats.

- Relax. If you are relaxed at your party, your guests will be too.

Chapter Seven

Living
with Color

COLOR IN THE FAMILY

Living with color makes a home visually joyful. Seize the opportunity and add joyful color to your home. Homes are about families of every description, and growing up living with color is a wonderful enhancement to a child's rearing. Take the lead from your children and their openness to new things, and decorate your home and life colorfully.

Children's rooms are a great place to start decorating. From the arrival of a baby to the teenage years, children's rooms probably receive as much decorating attention as any room. As children change and grow, their taste and style reinvents itself.

Children are naturally open to bright and colorful expression; subtle tones and neutrality are lost on their eager eyes. When I questioned my son Kelly's memory about color, he said, "I remember that if anything was bright and colorful I wanted to touch it, whether it was a toy, clothing, books or food, color drew my attention. Even colorful candy was more intriguing than chocolate."

Homes are about families of every description, and growing up living with color is a wonderful enhancement to a child's rearing.

Children, like nectar-seeking birds, are drawn to color.

Teenagers decorate their walls with posters; they fill their wall space with vivid renderings of their favorite ideas and people; they decorate, experiment and develop their ideas of living and space. Take a page from the teenagers' style guide—put stuff on your walls! You probably don't want a current poster of a hip-hop singer, but vintage posters are indeed collectible, nostalgic, often beautifully designed and can look good as a thematic series in a room. My oldest son Cameron collects vintage James Bond posters that add interest and art to his bohemian décor. Posters, like framed textiles, will add bold color to your décor.

To begin decorating a child's room, a formula I think is great is what I call reverse decorating. Try it for a child's room with twin beds. Even if you have only one child, having an extra bed for friends to sleep over is a great way to encourage company and helps make sure the action happens at your home. The reverse decorating technique is doing the beds in two different colors—say red and blue, then putting the red cushions and pillows on the blue bed and the blue ones on the red. Reverse out the matching blankets on the bottom of the beds to the other bed. The only real trick is that both groups should be of equal color value.

What does equal color value mean? It means that if the palette is light, all colors should be light, if dark, all dark and if medium, all medium. The reason for this is that if one color is much stronger than the other, the look will be unbalanced. Having both colors of equal value will balance the room. This same reverse decorating idea can be used for doing a series of tables for a garden party.

A girl's room can have lots of details. Have fun adorning walls with hanging hats or favorite purses. Children love pictures of animals; choose some artistically rendered animals and hang them too.

Never underestimate the impression of style on a child. I remember the room with twin beds I shared with my sister. It had wallpaper in lemon yellow with sketched Parisian

Colorful Concept

STORE IT OUT!

Don't hide your pretty things in a cupboard. Stack blankets on a dresser. Gather napkins in a basket. Pile placemats on a sideboard. Place a stack of color-coordinated tablecloths on an open shelf. Put plates and pretty bowls and jugs out on display on a plate rail. Store it out!

A row of dolls and stuffed animals on a child's bed says luxury in their language.

poodles sitting at a bistro table sipping lemonade in front of a sign that read café. Little did my mother know I would recall her charming choice many years later.

Children love pictures of themselves as babies. A framed photo of your child as a baby will be treasured. You may consider framing a christening gown or baby shoes for their walls. A row of dolls and stuffed animals on a child's bed says luxury in their language. The same way we love to pile pillows on our beds, children love to do the same with animals and dolls. It makes them feel "rich" and like they have a lot of friends.

LEFT: *This bright child's room illustrates a decorating term I call "reverse decorating."*

My oldest son Cameron, now 27, was reared in our colorful international life. He has grown up to love color, décor and design. He currently designs uncommon men's wear and I have to think his exposure at home led him to it. So show your children what you love, they will surely absorb your influence.

BOYS AND GIRLS

Symbolic color is not only the seasonal colors of red at Christmastime and pastels at Easter. It is also the pink and blue segregation of little girls and little boys. I think it starts with bald babies and mothers who want to be sure that there is no doubt about the gender of their child. Whatever it is, there are few parents who will give their boy a pink room.

ABOVE: *All my boys. Kelly, Lee, Cameron and Chris.*
RIGHT: *My boys have enjoyed many happy days and nights in this blue-hued room.*

Point of Inspiration

PUT ON COLOR

Here is a fun party idea—have a cooking party. Buy or make a range of colorful aprons. Everybody makes their best dish, and chooses their favorite colored apron to wear. Over food, you can discuss color— what attracted each person to their apron, why they like that color of print or that color of plaid. These color conversations are like a design focus group; they get you talking about color ideas and listening to other's ideas too. What a fun way to spend an after-noon with friends.

I have three sons so lace, frills and colors of the pink persuasion were not for them. At our lake house, there is a boys' room all in shades of boy blue. Plaids and stripes are considered masculine and a combination of these mixed with a border print in tonal blues adds depth to this simple palette. At the foot of the beds are patchwork quilts that add extra color and warmth. A framed print of wild ducks and a Quebecois pine dresser complete the simple décor. It is the combina-tion of blue colors that makes the room. There are no curtains so the light streams in, bringing the day inside. At night, wooden blinds lower for late-morning sleep-ins. Many a boy has had a cozy night in this room, curled under the warm cotton quilts or stretched out on a mattress on the floor. They felt as loved and cared for as any little girl in her pink room, but with an acceptably boyish motif.

When one of my sons, Lee, left home for college, I was putting together some bedding for him. I started hauling out some old tow-els and polyester sheets and was shocked to hear Lee say, "Mom, I want the nice colorful cotton sheets like we have at home." I guess he noticed!

WHERE COLOR COMES FROM

With so much talk about color you may be thinking that everything needs to be covered up, decorated and layered. Not so. Look at a wooden table waxed to a fine glow and see its rich color. Don't cover it up, highlight it with a cloth that is smaller than the table and leaves warm expanses of wood showing. Highlight wooden chairs with vibrant cushions, but allow the wood backs to show. Remember, color is coming from many places: floors, walls, light and the furnishings.

You can be simple and colorful, or you can be detailed and colorful. You can have various rooms with different degrees of decorating complexity. Learn to use different formulas in your home to capture different styles. When you want a simple look, use highlights of color. When you want a full look, use layers of color.

When you want a simple look, use highlights of color. When you want a full look, use layers of color.

COLOR AROUND THE HOUSE

"Wherever you are, there it is." Whoever said that, it is so true! When you start to live with color, you will soon find that wherever you are, there it is—color. If you saw my laundry you would know what I mean. There is no mistaking the color in my life. A peek in the trunk of my car will show a colorful shawl and an embroidered jacket, and the luggage is black with a bold print. Color follows me. I get pleasure when I hang a tablecloth over a rail or hang a blouse on a laundry line. Colorful tea towels in a bucket form a tableau that is as vividly engaging as a Rajasthani woman in a colorful costume, with swinging hips and a brass pot on her head. We create our own artful moments.

In a Nutshell

- Take the lead from children's love of color.

- Try reverse decorating for a multicolored room.

- Color can be a striking accent in a simple environment.

- Color can be surrounding and suffusing in a "layered" decorating scheme.

- Your family will learn color and decorating at the foot of their mother. Begin now!

- Let color permeate your life.

- Color adds beauty to everyday activities.

Old cultures show us that our daily lives can indeed show beauty and give inspiration. Live with color and you will make your own art.

For every chef, there is a favorite recipe, for every designer there is a favorite palette. You will naturally be drawn to favorite colors; enjoy these colors and make them your own. Learning to appreciate other colors will be part of your color recognition journey.

Chapter Eight

Now It's Your Turn

NATURE'S GIFT TO YOU

Being an artist doesn't mean you can draw; being an artist means you can see. And that is what this book is all about—being aware of color and bringing it into your life.

By now, you know how often I am inspired by color every day. It is a wonderful gift from nature, just waiting to be shared and enjoyed. All too often, we give in to the temptation of staying so closely focused on the tasks at hand that we don't get out and partake of the vibrant colorful world around us. I am confident that if you do—and take heed of my suggestions to bring nature's colors into your own home—you will have joy in the hours you spend there. The blends and contrasts of the colors of nature belong together—by direct dictate from Mother Nature.

If you are still hesitant and a bit uneasy about being bold with color, remember, nature didn't blend beiges or try to match each blue to blue. Oh, if she did, we would not recognize that world. So often people tell me that it's easy for me to see color because I am an artist. It insinuates that others can't see the same things too. I argue that it is chiefly a matter of awareness. Being an artist doesn't mean you can draw; being an artist means you can see. And that is what this book is all about—being aware of color and bringing it into your life. As with most good things, you may have to make a little effort. I assure you that it will be enjoyable.

A COMMITMENT TO COLOR

I have so enjoyed sharing my thoughts and experiences about color. Through this book we have been on a bit of a color journey. I hope it has been a joyful voyage. As with many experiences, it is good to look back and see where you have been.

OPPOSITE PAGE: Rock-a-bye baby! Placemats act as chair backs on these cheerful wooden rockers and marry the merry colors of the rockers and the pretty prints.

I offer this summary of the key points we have discussed:

Get Up and go!

Go outside. Make a date with yourself, go for a walk and see what you find in a natural setting. If you need an easy way out, go to a farmer's market and spend time perusing the fruit, produce and flowers. What colors do you see?

Recall a Color Memory

Take some quiet time and remember your first memory of color. Was it the color of your childhood room, the color of a favorite dress or perhaps your mother's blouse? Maybe it was laundry waving in a breeze against a blue summer sky or bright Christmas wrappings under a tree. Color memory is the day you knew that blue was blue and that clouds move and are not a landscape. Color memory is the day you became aware that you are a participant in the world of color. Whatever your memory is, try to think about what provoked your attention, what drew you to it and why.

Live only with beauty.

Begin to Build a Color Palette

Begin with a color you like and build on it. Using what you've seen on your nature walks, find accent colors and then find contrast colors.

Use your color journal to remind yourself of the colors you love. Move the colors around in your palette until you feel comfortable with them. Let them sing to you! When you decorate you will be singing back.

Start by Adding Small Touches

A tablecloth, a throw, even a favorite jacket over the back of sofa is a great way to begin to introduce color into your home. Don't forget one of my favorite ways to get quick color—frame a fabric you like.

Live Only with Beauty

It is time to treat yourself to beauty. Remove anything from your home that does not have special meaning or is not beautiful to you. We tend to hang onto useless things that bother us every time we walk by. Remove them and collect things you admire and that inspire you.

Choose Your Colors

Color is a very personal thing; it appeals to each of us in a slightly different way. Once you feel that you know what colors you prefer and feel comfortable with, you'll begin to see that they almost attract themselves to you. You'll find that when shopping or browsing, you'll feel automatically drawn to the colors and combination of colors you have chosen for your own palette. Use your colors.

Make a Mood with Color

Remember that color affects mood in many ways. Much of the response is based on our memories and the things we relate to

RIGHT: *Train your eye to see details, colors and texture, then step back and see the big picture. Now you can critique your décor and pull it all together.*

different colors. Personally, I enjoy many color moods. The clean glistening colors of the tropics, the comforting contrasts of the forest in autumn and the soft pastels of spring, all appeal to me, yet I feel differently when surrounded by each one. Think about the mood you want.

Work Color into Your Life

Begin with simple ways of adding color to your décor. Try paint first. Choose several colors you like and paint a small portion of the wall with each one. Once you have viewed it in different light at different times of the day, you will know which one is right. Then go for it! Get some color on those walls. Colorful cushions can brighten a room in minutes. Try simple colorful window coverings and then, as you feel comfortable, move on to furniture and accessories. Oh, and remember, don't get caught up in the matching game—blend and contrast.

Entertain in Color

Share your joy of color with others by being sure to entertain in vivid, glorious

Inspired Uses

Today, many women have their own desk and it is not always the traditional office-style desk. I think a desk should suit the need. If it is a desk for writing cards, journaling and making notes, it should be as attractive as the activity.

The orange and gold madras voile curtains above the desk shown here create a nice contrast to the rich wood of the desk. Two chairs with different cushions speak of style and casualness. Note the contrast of fabrics in the cushions, one is a rich silk brocade the other a cotton. These are a good example of coordinating by keeping the color theme without matching. The color of the desk also forms a part of the color theme.

color. Try layering tablecloths in different colors and patterns. Bring color to the table with dishes, glassware and, of course, food! Flowers do the job of adding nature and color in a vase. How easy is that!

Don't Forget the Ambience

You can use the most wonderful colors and set a delightful table or decorate a charming room, but if you don't tend to the details that create ambience, color won't have nearly the impact it should. Remember lighting, candles, flowers and favorite accessories that personalize your home.

I hope my love for color has been infectious and that you have been able to begin to see your world through clear eyes that return the world in all its vibrant color to you. I've enjoyed sharing my love of color with you.

Dear friends, I wish you a happy, wonderful, colorful life!

LEFT: *Be bountiful at breakfast. Breakfast is a meal that all family members enjoy; fill them up with good food and good conversation.*

In a Nutshell

Dear Friend,

Take the colors of the sky, the leaves, the flowers, the earth and the seasons; mix them with the colors from ourselves, take all the colors around you and distill them in a book. Then, my friend, when you are ready, your colors will be there. Faithful to your finding, they patiently await the day you open up their richness to beautify your home.

Enjoy your life with color as a friend.

Sincerely,

Amit

Acknowledgments

Many thanks to the Bark Lake team: Chris Cornell for styling and cooking; Robin Gronlund for coordinating many aspects of this book; Eileen Paulin, Jo Packham and Sara Toliver for creative styling; Dick O'Shaughnessy, artist and woodsman for wonderful support and back woods know-how; Mick Hales for dawn-to-dusk photography.

Many thanks to the Cayman Island team: Mario Garcia for his great hand with flowers and foliage and his wonderful shoe napkin; Chris Cornell for styling, island-style; Hesseline and Paula for Caribbean food and support; Courtney Platt for colorful photography.

Many thanks to the California team: Amber Volk and Betty Volk for organizing and propping, styling and smiling; Eileen Paulin, Rebecca Ittner and Jayne Cosh for creative styling and displays; Photographer Mark Tanner for his mellow California shots.

Many thanks to my mother Florence Janbroers for ideas and brainstorming and her love of decorating.

Many thanks to Wendy Lee Fiset for helping me organize my ideas—and enjoy happy accidents.

Many thanks to Bob and Cindy Ellis for opening their home, and Deborah Harmon for her hospitality.

Many thanks to Caroline Teo, photographer, and to Carrie Bilodeau for assisting me.

Many thanks to Barbara Carpenter for her daily support.

Many thanks to Deborah Kehoe for book design—a person as moved and inspired by color as myself.

Index

April Cornell Store List

UNITED STATES

ALABAMA

Birmingham
The Summit
(205) 970-1660

ARIZONA

Scottsdale
Kierland Commons
(480) 607-7790

Tucson
La Encantada
(520) 615-9869

CALIFORNIA

Berkeley
1774 Fourth Street
(510) 527-0715

Corte Madera
Village at Corte Madera
(415) 924-5880

La Jolla
1000 Prospect Avenue
(858) 454-1980

Newport Beach
Fashion Island Shopping
Center
(949) 721-9061

Palm Desert
The Gardens on El Paseo
(760) 341-8372

Pasadena
340 East Colorado Blvd.
(626) 440-7253

Sacramento
Arden Fair Mall
(916) 925-5940

San Diego
Fashion Valley Center
(619) 298-8482

Santa Barbara
301 Paseo Nuevo
(805) 899-4689

Santa Clara
Valley Fair Mall
(408) 261-9970

Walnut Creek
1180 Broadway Plaza
(925) 939-2437

COLORADO

Boulder
1123 Pearl Street
(303) 442-3723

Broomfield
Flat Iron Crossing
(303) 439-2179

Denver
Cherry Creek Shopping Center
(303) 316-9898

CONNECTICUT

Danbury
Danbury Fair Mall
(203) 791-1137

Farmington
West Farms Mall
(860) 521-1923

Greenwich
92 Greenwich Avenue
(203) 661-3563

FLORIDA

Miami
The Falls Shopping Center
(305) 254-2204

Palm Beach
The Gardens of the Palm
Beaches
(561) 625-6979

Tampa
Old Hyde Park Village
(813) 251-3019

GEORGIA

Atlanta
Lenox Square Mall
(404) 812-1722
Perimeter Mall
(770) 671-0722

Agusta
3450 Wrightsboro Road
(706) 667-9442
Perimeter Mall
(770) 671-0722

Norcross
The Forum Shopping Center
(770) 447-8021

ILLINOIS

Deer Park
20530 N. Rand Rd.
(847) 540-5909

Geneva
Geneva Commons
(630) 845-0074

Northbrook
Northbrook Court
(847) 564-8570

Oakbrook
Oakbrook Center
(630) 574-3066

INDIANA

Indianapolis
Keystone Fashion Mall West
(317) 569-9289

MARYLAND

Annapolis
16 Marketspace
(410) 263-4532

Baltimore
The Gallery at Harbor Place
(410) 234-0050

Columbia
The Mall in Columbia
(410) 730-9007

Hagerstown
Hagerstown Prime Outlets
(301) 790-1313

Towson
Towson Town Center
(410) 823-0833

MASSACHUSETTS

Boston
Faneuil Hall Marketplace
(617) 248-0280

Cambridge
43 Brattle Street
(617) 661-8910

Newton
The Mall at Chestnut Hill
(617) 965-1126

Wrentham
Wrentham Premium Outlets
(508) 384-9538

MICHIGAN

Lansing
Eastwood Towne Center
(517) 485-7940

Troy
Somerset Collection North
(248) 816-9660

MINNESOTA

Edina
The Galleria Mall
(952) 836-0830 MISSOURI

Kansas City
Country Club Plaza
(816) 960-0333

St. Louis
Saint Louis Galleria
(314) 725-0120

NEW HAMPSHIRE

North Conway
Settlers' Green
(603) 356-0820

NEW JERSEY

Bridgewater
Bridgewater Commons
(908) 218-9699

Princeton
51 Palmer Square West
(609) 921-3559

Short Hills
The Mall at Short Hills
(973) 258-0660

Shrewsbury
The Grove at Shrewsbury
(732) 758-0066

NEW YORK

Central Valley
Woodbury Common
(845) 928-4885

Ithaca
The Commons
(607) 277-5515

New York
487 Columbus Avenue
(212) 799-4342

Waterloo

Waterloo Premium Outlets

(315) 539-0140

NORTH CAROLINA

Raleigh

Crabtree Valley Mall

(919) 781-7817

Triangle Town Center

(919) 792-2820

OHIO

Cincinnati

Kenwood Town Centre

(513) 936-8819

Lyndhurst

Legacy Village

(216) 382-7190

OREGON

Portland

Pioneer Place

(503) 222-2171

PENNSYLVANIA

Ardmore

Suburban Square

(610) 642-9540

King of Prussia

Court of King of Prussia

(610) 265-0317

Philadelphia

The Shops at Liberty Place

(215) 981-0350

SOUTH CAROLINA

Charleston

Charleston Place

(843) 805-7000

Greenville

Greenville Mall

(864) 234-9667

TENNESSEE

Memphis

Oak Court Mall

(901) 767-9110

TEXAS

Austin

The Arboretum

(512) 345-9908

Dallas

1014 North Park Center

(214) 750-8338

River Oaks

Shopping Center

(713) 520-0426

Plano

The Shops at Willow Bend

(972) 202-5536

VERMONT

Burlington

87 Church Street

(802) 862-8211

VIRGINIA

Arlington

Fashion Centre at Pentagon City

(703) 415-2290

Charlottesville

Barracks Road

Shopping Center

(434) 295-9121

McLean

Tysons Corner Center

(703) 448-6972

Norfolk

MacArthur Center

(757) 625-5804

Richmond

Stony Point Fashion Park

(804) 330-7053

WASHINGTON

Bellevue

215 Bellevue Square

(425) 455-9818

Seattle

West Lake Center

(206) 749-9658

WASHINGTON D.C.

3278 M Street NW

(202) 625-7887

WISCONSIN

Wauwsatosa

2500 N. Mayfair Road

(414) 476-8776

CANADA

ALBERTA

Banff

Cascade Plaza

(403) 760-3974

Calgary

South Centre Mall

(403) 271-3536

Scotia Centre

(403) 263-5545

Edmonton

W. Edmonton Mall

(780) 481-2038

Southgate Mall

(780) 437-9406

BRITISH COLUMBIA

Vancouver

2956 Granville Street

(604) 731-8343

Victoria

Eaton Centre

(250) 384-6343

West Vancouver

Park Royal North Shopping Centre

(604) 926-3250

NOVA SCOTIA

Halifax

Park Lane Mall

(902) 423-1844

ONTARIO

Hamilton

Jackson Square Mall

(905) 528-3270

Kingston

208 Princess Street

(613) 544-0905

London

White Oaks Mall

(519) 680-7412

Newmarket

17600 Yonge Street

(905) 836-9158

Ottawa

763 Bank Street

(613) 233-0412

Toronto

346 Queen Street West

(416) 979-8140

2619 Yonge Street

(416) 482-8480

2264 Bloor Street West

(416) 760-7592

PRINCE EDWARD ISLAND

Charlottetown

Confederation Court Mall

(902) 569-5716

QUEBEC

Hudson

425 rue Principale

(450) 458-1717

Laval

Carrefour Laval

(450) 973-9961

Montréal

108 Gallery Square

(514) 846-1091

3941 rue St-Denis

(514) 842-7693

Place Montreal Trust

(514) 847-5307

Mt-Tremblant

118 ch. Kandahar

(819) 681-6363

Outremont

1051 rue Laurier Ouest

(514) 273-9700

Pte-Claire

Fairview

(514) 426-1616

Ste-Foy

Place de la Cité

(418) 651-1305

Vieux-Quebec

1150 rue St-Jean

(418) 692-0398

Westmount

1353 Avenue Greene

(514) 935-4361

www.aprilcornell.com